Animals

A
for Adults

illustrated by Rachel Jones

FREE BONUS PAGES
Visit: http://racheljonesarts.com/animals/ to receive a PDF of 5 bonus coloring pages.

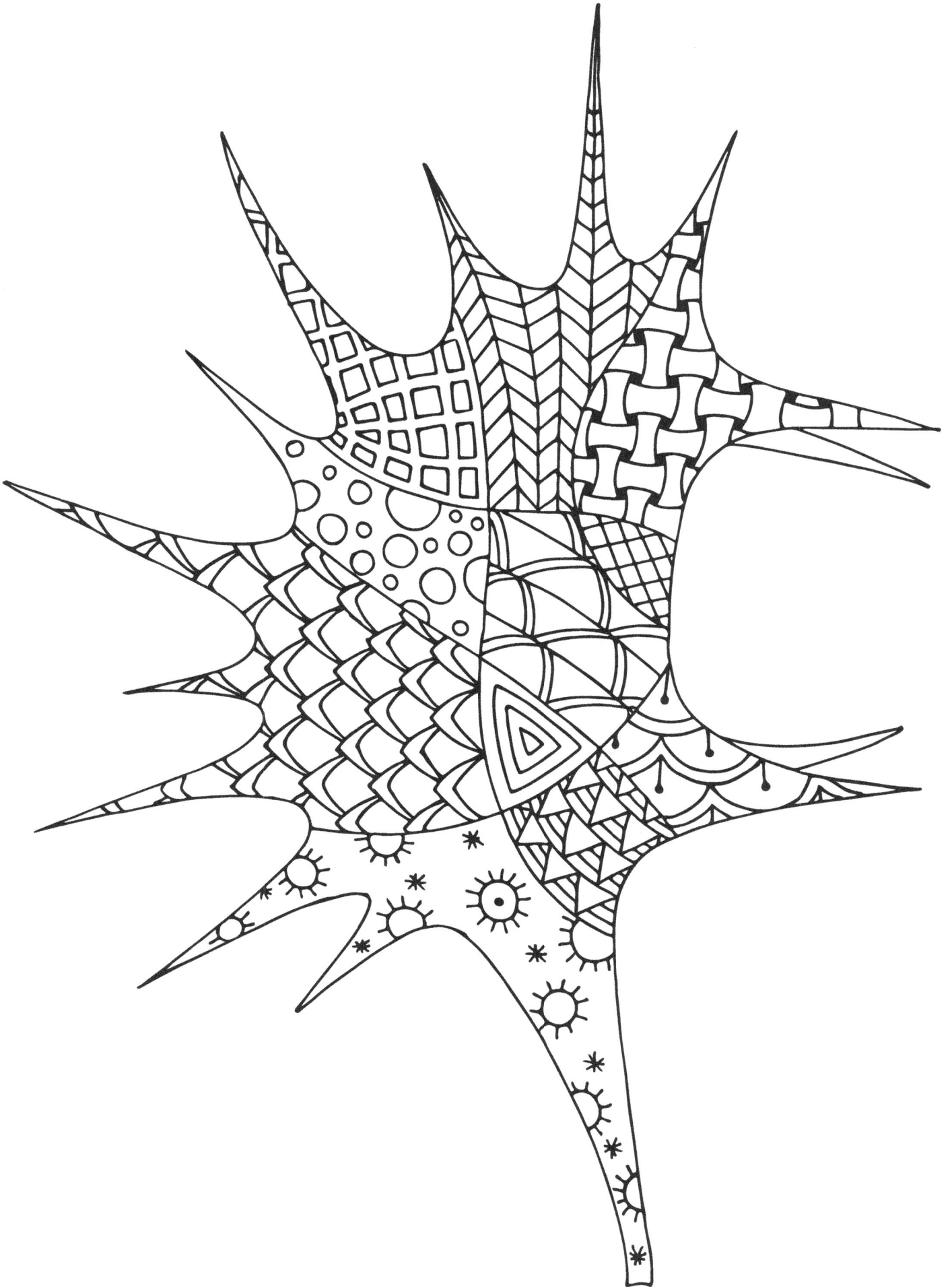

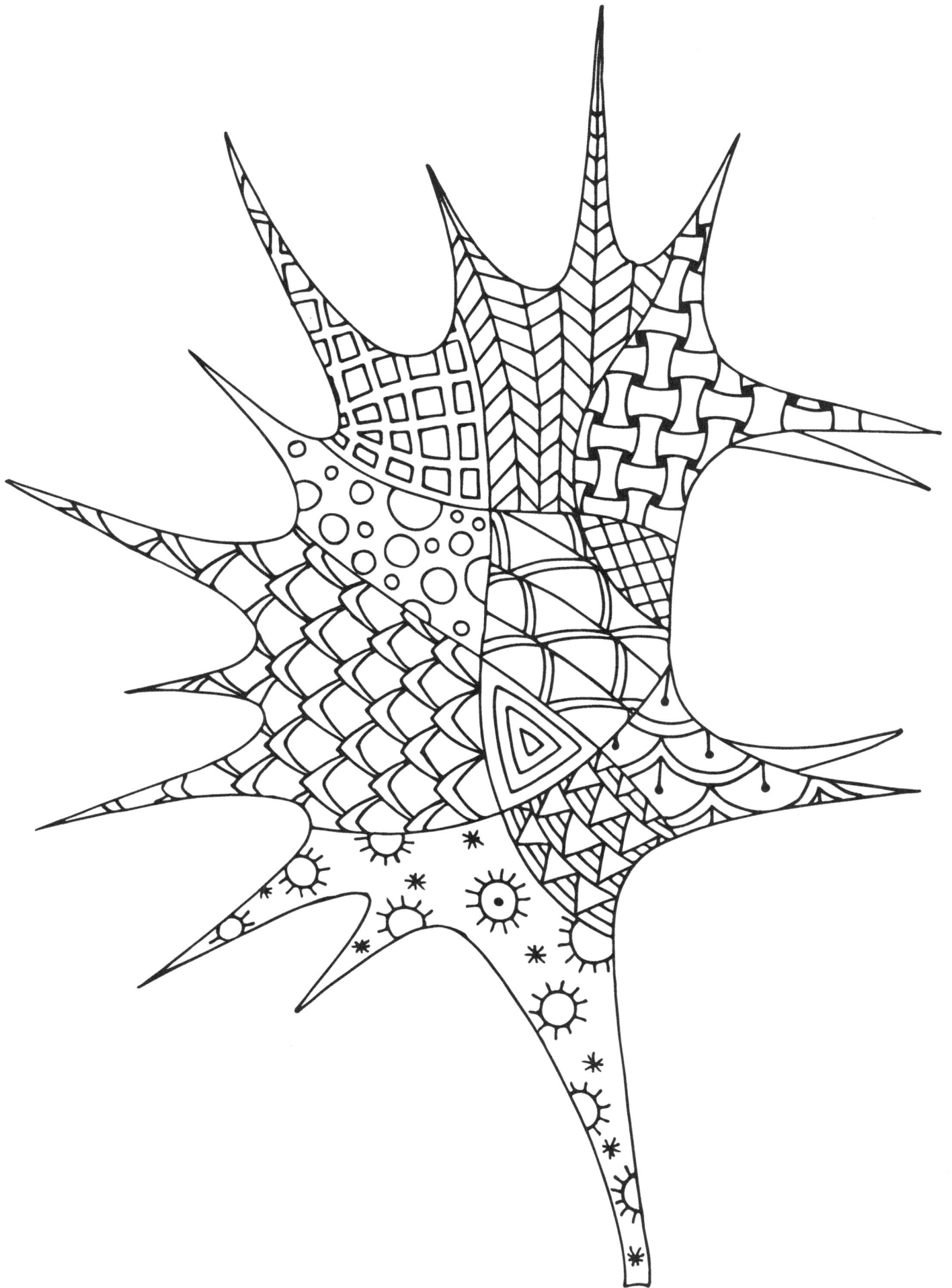

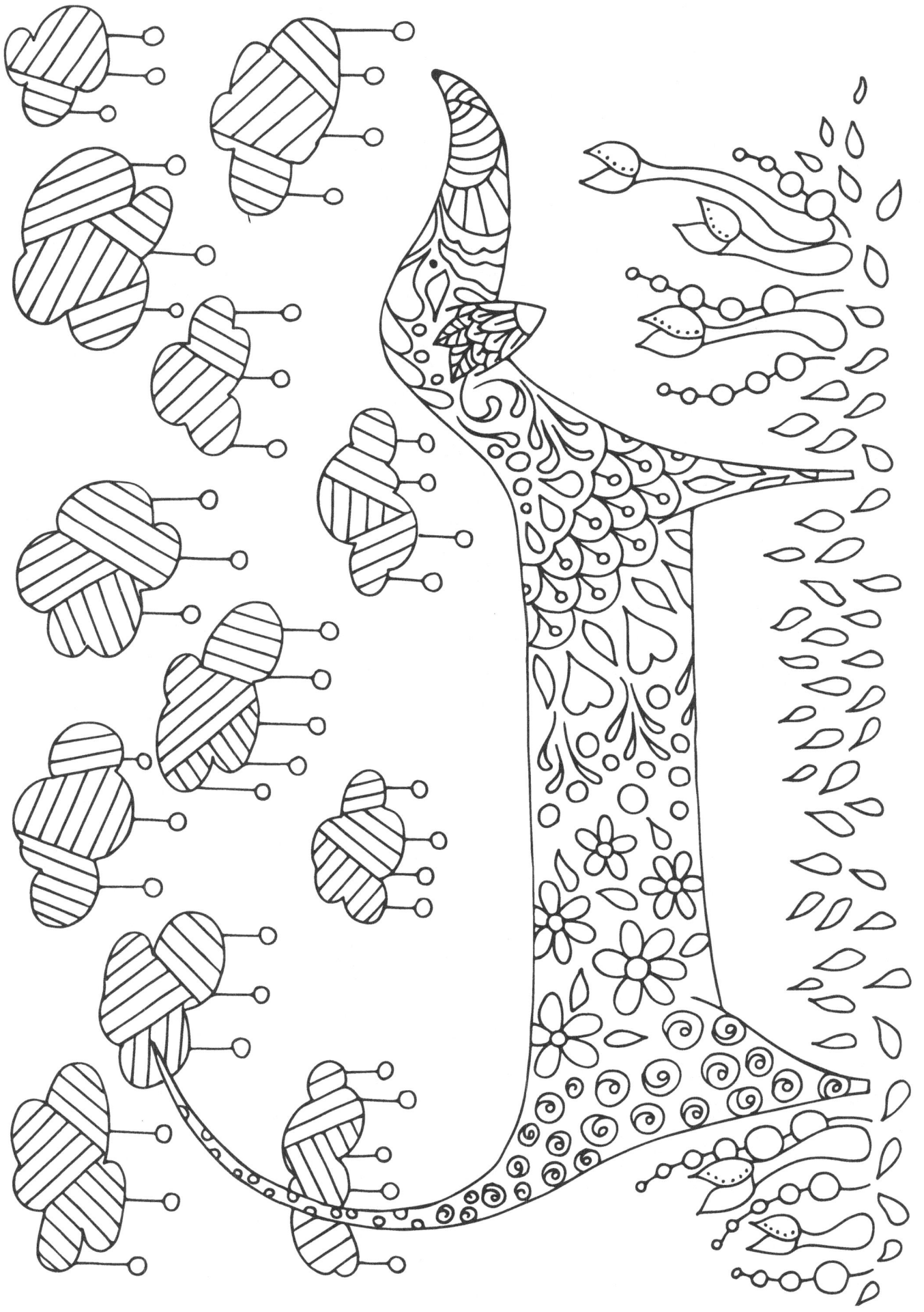

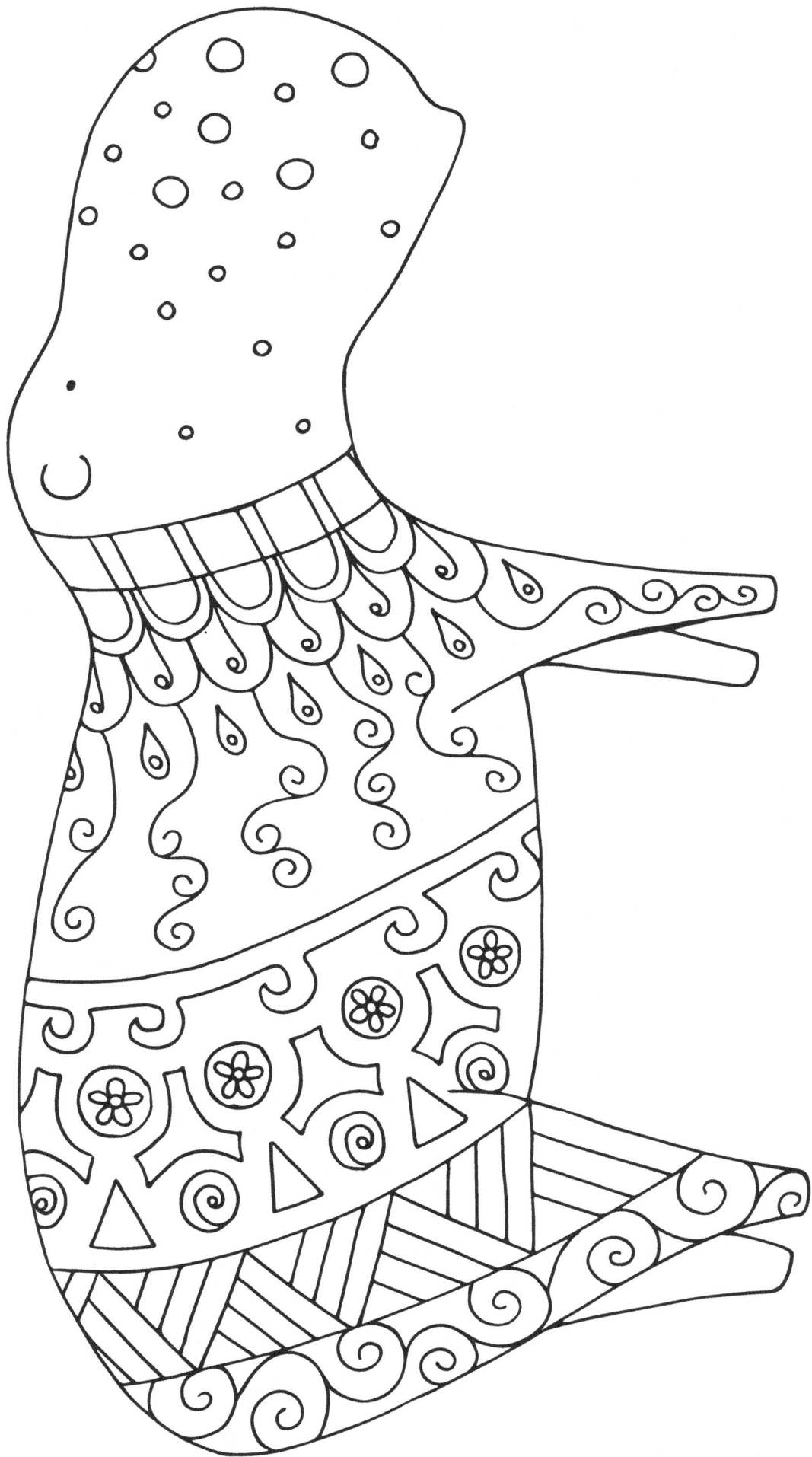

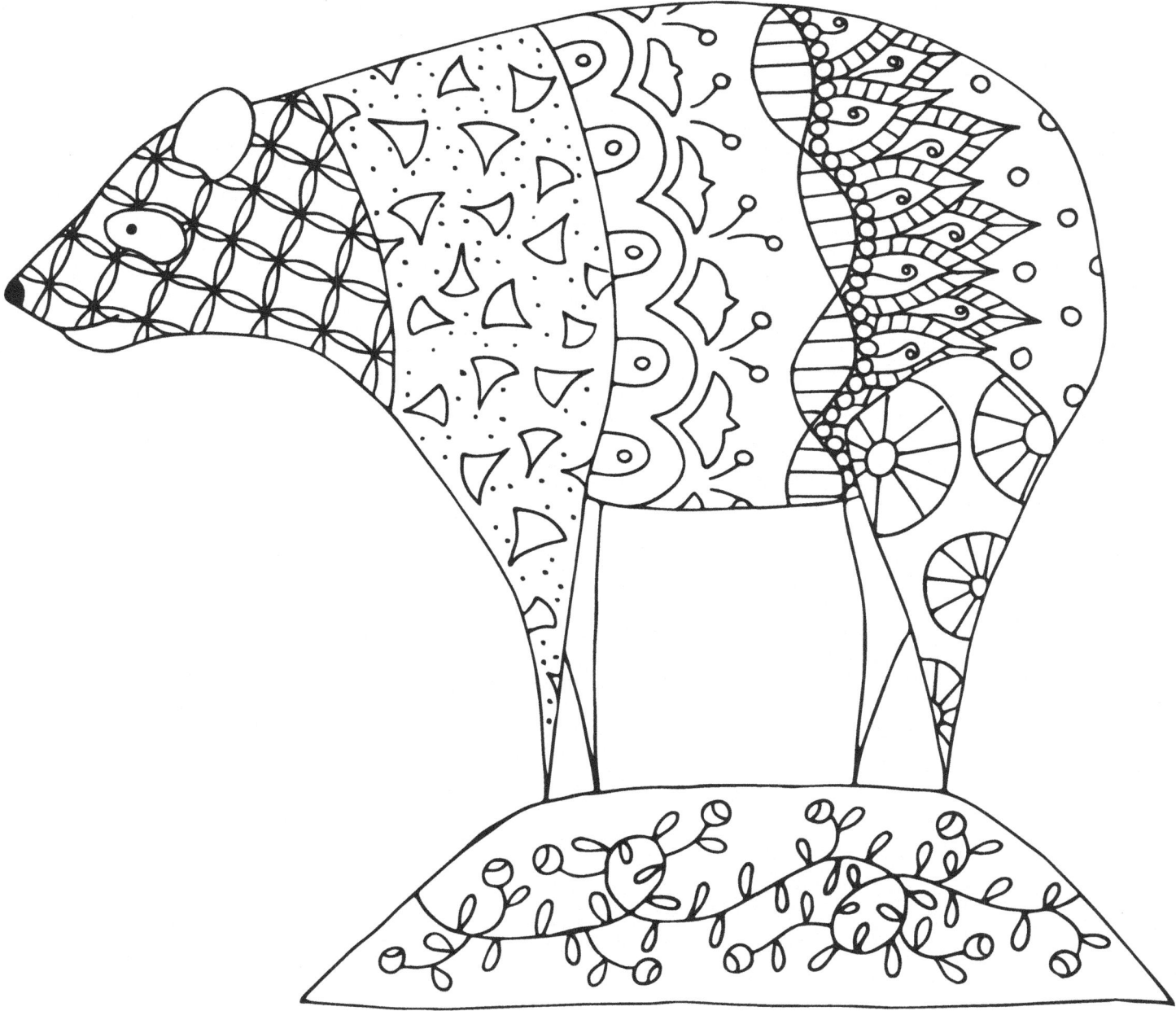

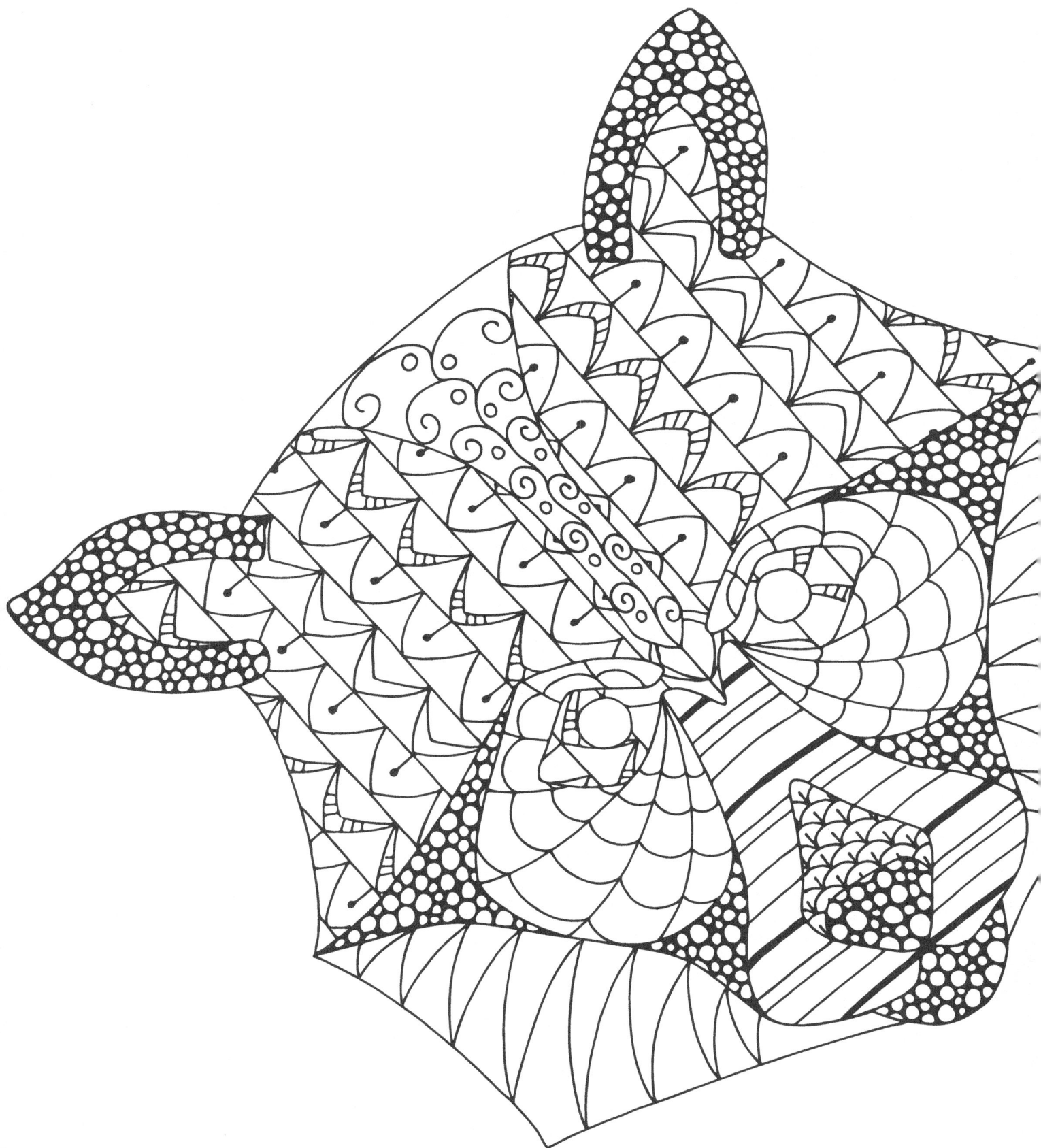

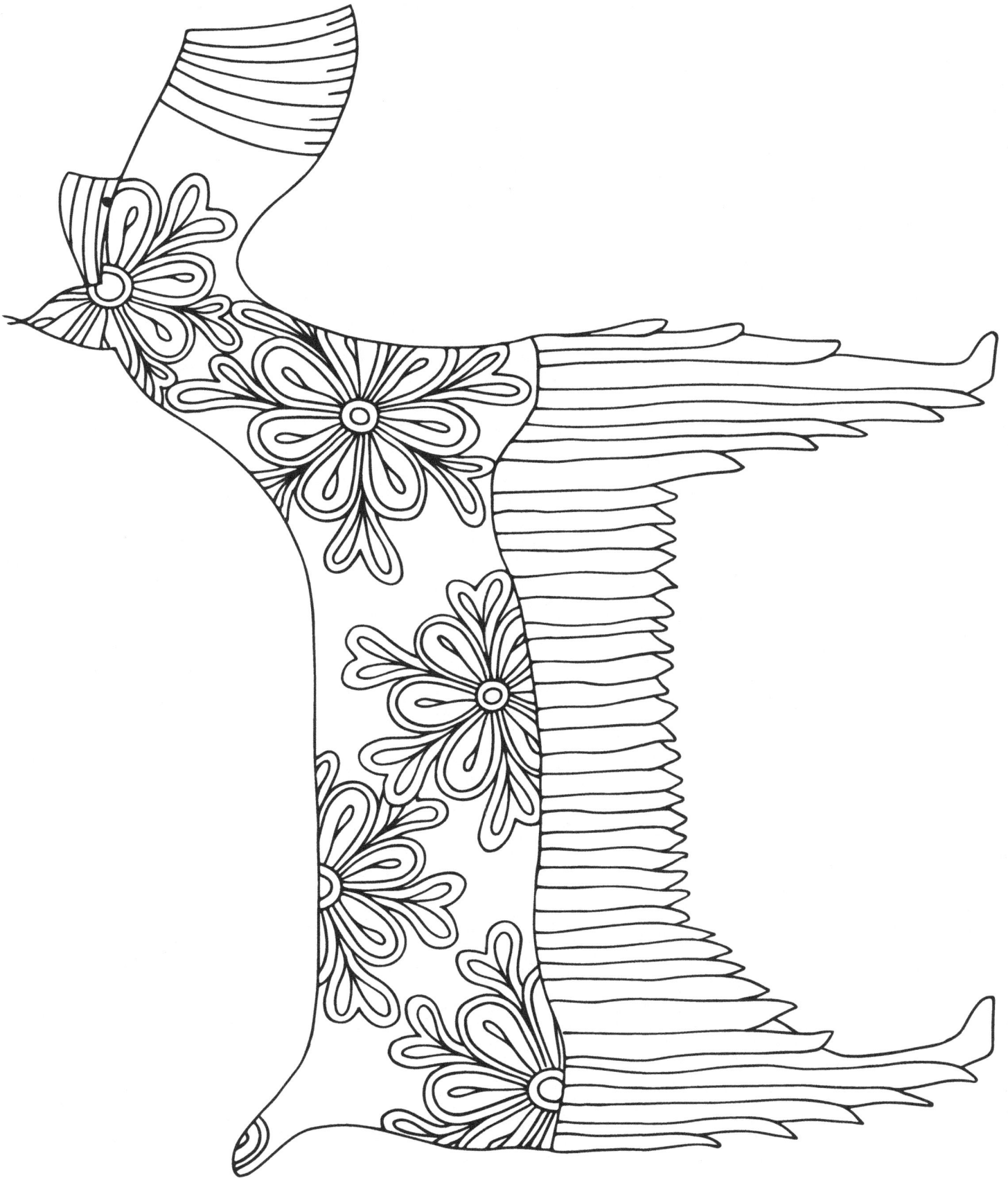

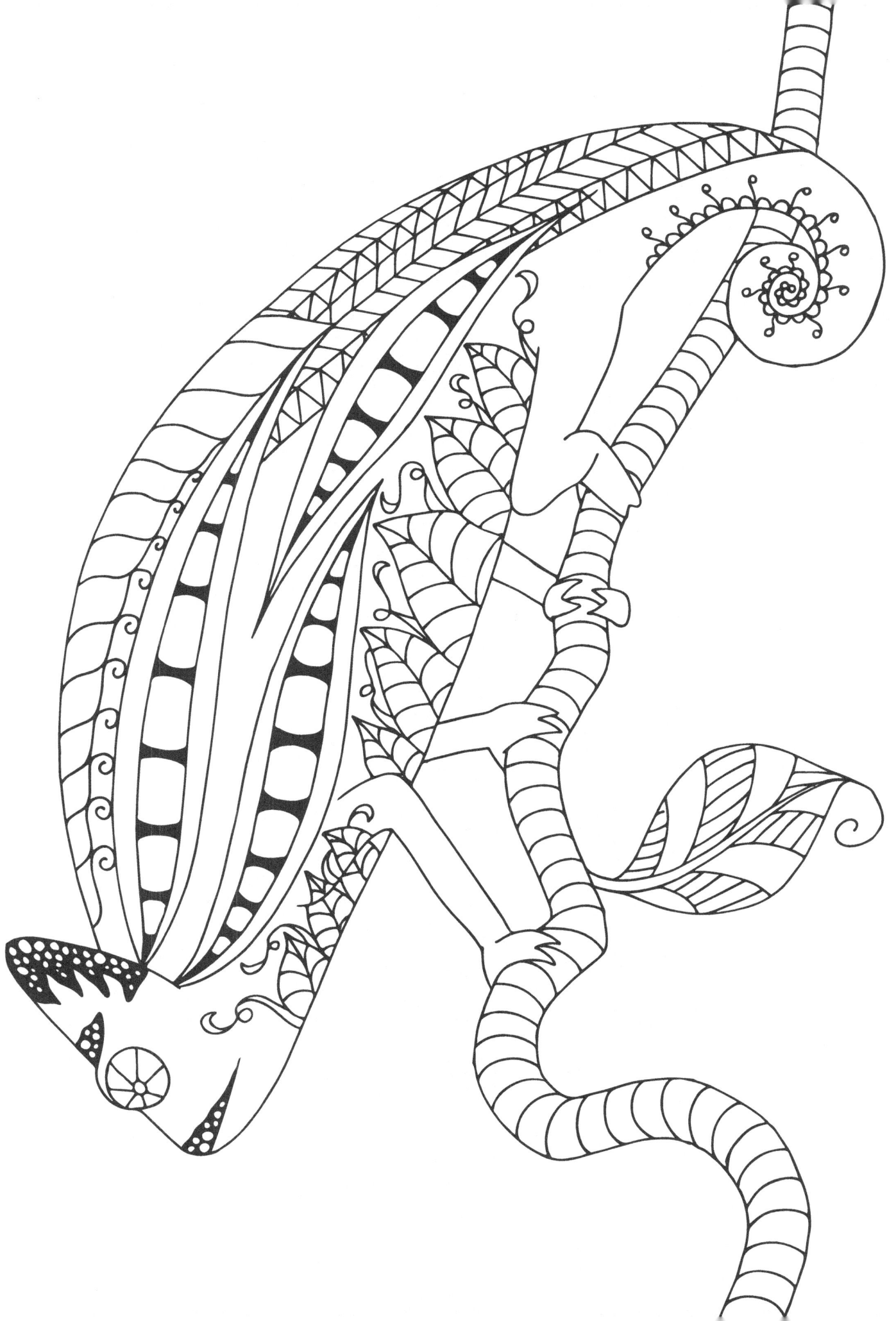

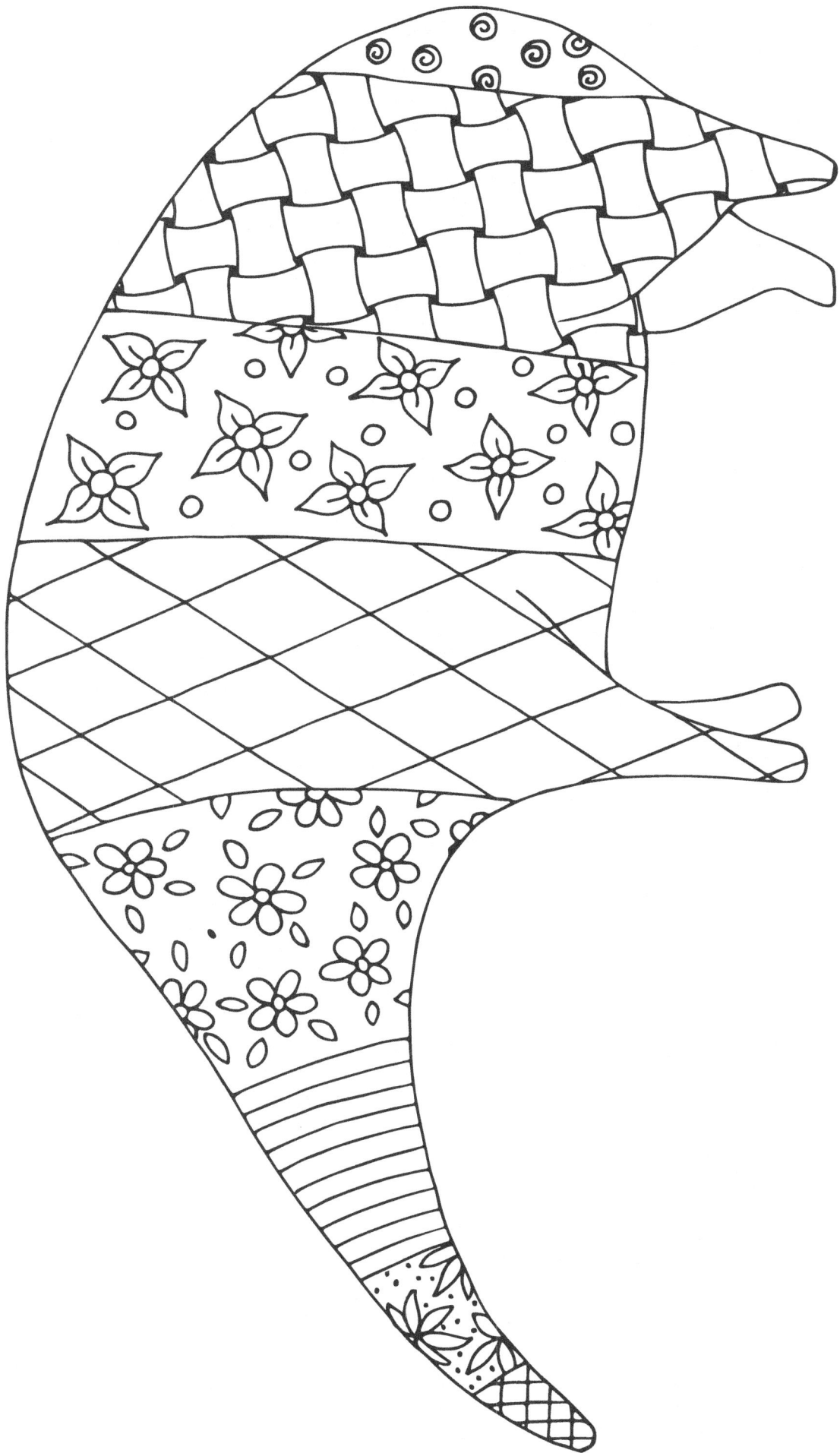

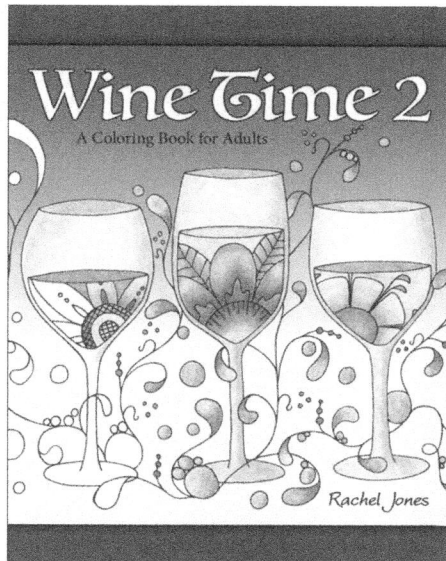

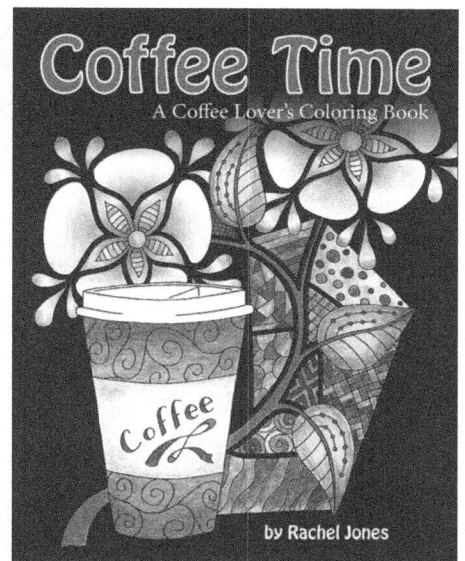

Get more coloring books at RachelJonesArts.com

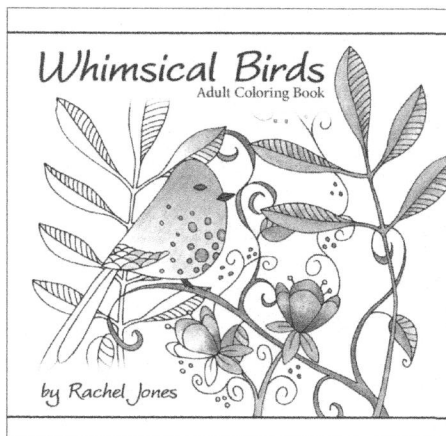

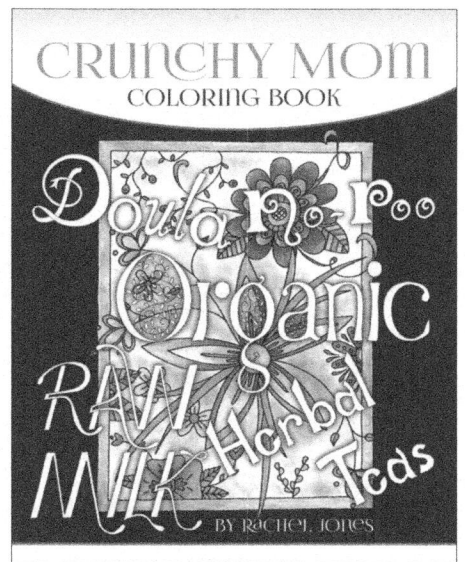

Made in the USA
Las Vegas, NV
14 December 2023